Real Vermonters
Don't
Milk Goats

Real Vermonters Don't Milk Goats

by
Frank Bryan
and
Bill Mares

Illustrations by Howard Johnson

The New England Press
Shelburne, Vermont

First printing, September 1983
Second printing, October 1983
Third printing, December 1983

For additional copies write to:

The New England Press, Inc.
P. O. Box 575
Shelburne, Vermont 05482

Library of Congress Card Catalog Number: 83–61500
ISBN: 0–933050–16–X

ACKNOWLEDGMENTS

Many people have contributed to this book. We would like to thank Chuck Bann, Tom Bassett, David Bryan, Hamilton Davis, Ed Ducharme, Jan Feldman, Frank Hagerty, David Hale, Ann Hallowell, Barbara Hird, John McClaughry, Charlie Morrissey, Scudder Parker, Susan Pekala, Steve Wheelock, and Bill Wilson. We are especially indebted to our wives Lee Bryan and Chris Hadsel.

PRINTED IN THE UNITED STATES OF AMERICA

Good Fences
Make
Good Neighbors

I (Bill Mares) and I (Frank Bryan) believe in Frost's words. That is why we agreed to co-author this book only after a rigorous delineation of rights, duties, and responsibilities. I (Bryan) was worried about Bill's pines coming over into my apples. I (Mares) was worried about Frank's apples getting mixed up with my pines.

Bryan's name is first on the cover only because it starts with a "B" and Mares begins with an "M." I (Mares) offered to flip him for it. I (Bryan) felt Real Vermonters would expect alphabetical listing and suspect I was a secondary author. I (Mares), realizing that his (Bryan's) tenure decision was pending at the University of Vermont, was polite enough not to call him (Bryan) a jackass.[1]

Both of us felt it essential that you (the reader) understand that we split everything 50/50 and had erected, in true Vermont fashion, good solid fences between us before we began to cooperate. Since the work was precisely shared, the blame for the book must be equally divided between us.

We say this even though we know that as sure as the tamaracks turn orange in deer season . . . REAL VERMONTERS WON'T GIVE A DAMN!

[1]These negotiations took place over soup and a hamburger at the Oasis Diner, a Real Vermonter's hangout in downtown Burlington, a large city that has the advantage of being very close to the Vermont border.

Contents

1

East

of

Hardwick

It was one of those soggy April afternoons. We were on our way to Lyndonville where Frank was to debate the future of Town Meeting.

A late snow was retreating fast, leaving the land mangy and laced with dozens of little rivulets of funny colored water. Driveways were sliced with ruts. All that remained of woodpiles were wood chips and torn black plastic. On the few farms we passed, the cows stood knee-deep in mud, their winter coats hanging loose.

What snowbanks remained were like huge meteorites half-buried in the ground. Sprinkled about the lawns were alternating piles of ashes and dog manure. The face of Vermont was embarrassed, rotten with the residues of winter.

We prayed for darkness.

On a back road somewhere between Hardwick and Lyndon we slurped around a corner to see a neat two-story log cabin cut strategically into the bright side of a hill with a long view to the southwest. From the chimney wood-smoke rose cheerfully. The well-drained, crushed-rock driveway led to a carport and two vehicles, a 4WD pickup truck and a small Japanese station wagon.

A man and a woman and two small children were out surveying a turned-over plot, which was obviously their garden. Behind the house was a small barn perhaps twenty feet square. A perfect woodpile stood at attention by the garage waiting patiently for another winter.

"Looks like a fold-out from *Country Journal,*" Mares said.

"Flatlander," Bryan agreed.

"Oh, *really*?" Mares asked. "And what are we?"

"Speak for yourself. I've been here all my life. There were only seven students in my graduating class at Newbury High." Bryan was fairly glowing!

"But were you *born* here?" Mares bored in.

Professor Bryan is not often short of words, but several seconds passed before he choked an almost inaudible "No."

"Then you're not a *Real* Vermonter," Mares's voice rose in triumph. "You're an outsider . . . just like me!"

Bryan didn't give up.

"But I was conceived here! In Canaan! In the northernmost, easternmost town in the Northeast Kingdom."

"But where were you *born*?" asked Mares as relentless as a Chinese water torturer.

"West Stewartstown, New Hampshire. But . . . ."

"Then, of course, you're not a Real Vermonter. I suppose you support Edgar May's bill to doctor up birth certificates like yours. That might make you a Real Vermonter legally, Frank, but you and I will always know the truth.[1]

---

[1] Actually Bryan opposes the idea introduced to the Legislature by Edgar May of Springfield. Such a law would make it possible for people like former U V M President Lyman Rowell (and most of Bryan's friends back in Newbury who were born at the Cottage Hospital in Woodsville, New Hampshire) to become Real Vermonters by having their birth certificates indicate a Real Vermont Birth if their parents were living in Vermont at the time. "If we water down the definition," says Bryan, "pretty soon *everyone* will be claiming Real Vermonter status."

"I was brought to term here, damnit. The wind was blowing west to east when I emerged from the womb. The hospital was in sight of Vermont, on the banks of the Connecticut River. You can throw a dollar . . . ."

"Give up, Bryan. You're not a Real Vermonter."

"I was only there in the hospital a week. When my mother opened her room window, she could smell the hay drying on the Vermont side. It was June. I was back in Vermont in less than seven days. There wasn't another hospital within fifty miles. My parents were living in Vermont. They were both Real Vermonters."

"Were they born here?"

"You betcha."

"O.K. I'll accept that. But that doesn't make you one. By the way, Real Vermonters don't say, 'You betcha.'"

Bryan lapsed into silence as we drove northeast towards Lyndonville, his mood reflecting the landscape. Just before we came out onto Route 5 and the hardtop we passed another small neat house and barn. On the roadside was printed in bold if amateurish letters: **GOAT'S MILK FOR SALE.**

Bryan grunted. "REAL Vermonters don't milk goats."

"They don't eat quiche, either," Mares replied.

"Who *are* Real Vermonters?" Bryan asked, his mood brightening even as the day darkened.

"Hell, I don't know. But they don't have conversations like this and . . . ." Bill braced for a particularly bad rut. "And they have more sense than to take back roads in mud season."

"That's it!" Bryan exclaimed, happily grabbing for the dash as the car lurched crazily.

"Why not write a book about it?" Mares's question was more an assertion conditioned only by his hope that Bryan's enthusiasm was more authentic than his birthright.

"Yeah!"

And that's how it got started—East of Hardwick.

REAL VERMONTERS
DON'T RIDE THEIR
LAWNMOWERS...

THEY DON'T MILK THEM EITHER.

2

Real Vermonters Don't Wear L. L. Bean Boots

It gets more and more difficult to tell a Real Vermonter from a Flatlander. This is because many Flatlanders do their best to look like Real Vermonters. Here are some hints, however, that may help.

Real Vermonters don't wear bib overalls. They don't tie their sweaters around their necks. They wear hats when it's cold, even if they have wavy hair. They never wear heart shoelaces in their sneakers.

Real Vermonters don't wear hiking boots in town, headbands on the street, or running shoes when they walk.[1] You will *never* see a Real Vermonter in leather pants. Real Vermont men always keep their shirts buttoned up. Real Vermont women never wear "jog bras," even though they're made in Vermont. When Real Vermonters go hunting they never wear "hunter orange." They wear red.[2]

---

[1]Remember, of course, that Real Vermonters don't run. They figure if it is that important to get to, the hell with it.

[2]Real Vermonters *never* hunt with "hot seats" strapped on their hind sides.

A Real Vermonter's watch doesn't blink or buzz or play "Edelweiss." It doesn't tell the day of the week, the sum of 47 and 23, or the square root of 87. A Real Vermonter would never own a watch that incessantly flashed the time in fractions of a second. Dividing time into tenths of a second is, to a Real Vermonter, damn foolishness.

Real Vermonters get dressed up for church, weddings, funerals, and graduations. Real Vermonters don't have undershirts with writing on them. Real Vermonters, of course, always wear underwear.[3] Anyone seen at Town meeting in Levi's is not a Real Vermonter. They never try to look like farmers. They never have fur inside their gloves. They never wear cowboy hats or string ties. If you see a man with a hat on in July he is probably a Real Vermonter. Real Vermont women never carry plastic galoshes in their purses.

While Real Vermonters never walk in the rain, they do ride on tractors in the rain. Consequently, a good many Real Vermonters are wet a good deal of the time.

No one seen under an umbrella is ever a Real Vermonter. Anyone seen *carrying* an umbrella on the *suspicion* of rain is a quintessential Flatlander.

Most of all, Real Vermonters never, never try to look like Real Vermonters.[4]

[3] From October to May it is long underwear.
[4] Real Vermonters never try to look like Flatlanders either.

REAL VERMONTERS WON'T JOG,
BUT WILL RUN—IF PRESSED.

3

Questions a Real Vermonter Would Never Ask

Your car is stuck in a snowbank. It's zero outside and the wind is howling up a gale.

Just as your hope begins to fade, up drives a shiny "Bronco" or 'Renegade."[1] The driver jumps out to help.

"Boy, it's too cold to be stuck out here," you say.

"It sure is," this savior says. "I wonder what the wind chill factor is?"

Bingo! You know it's a Flatlander. If you listen carefully, you can hear other Flatlanders betray their origins by the questions they ask.

Here are some more:

- What's your sign?
- How deep do you plant them?
- Where does the sap come from?
- Where's a good place to picnic around here?
- Have you read *Real Vermonters Don't Milk Goats?*
- Where can I buy *The New York Times?*
- What's the "R" factor?
- How many BTU's does it generate?
- How big do the horns have to be?
- Where were you born?
- Do you have a view of the mountains?

---

[1] Real Vermonters drive no vehicles with macho names. They will accept the term "wagon," but only if it is attached to the word "station." And, every once in a great while, "Volks."

Real Vermonters don't say, "Let's see how this sugars off."

WOODCHUCK GROUNDHOG
☐ TRUE
☐ FALSE

4

The Real Vermonter Quiz # 1

Identify each of the following:

(a) throw up

(b) cant dog

(c) the Warning

(d) freshening

(e) whiffletree

(f) grand list

(g) Bag Balm

(h) stone boat

(i) daughter out

(j) bullin

(k) three titter

(l) short corded

(m) the "mountain rule"

(n) the "governor"

(o) meadow mayonnaise

(p) rowen

(q) jack jumper

(r) party permit

The correct answers are provided on page 89.

5
*The
Real Vermonter's
Sex Life*

Please turn to page 42.

The Real Vermonter Quiz # 2

(a) What is the Northeast Kingdom?

(b) How big is a cord of wood?

(c) What does "Winooski" mean in Abenaki?

(d) Where was Matthew Lyon living when he was elected to Congress from Vermont?

(e) Where did the St. Albans' raid take place?

(f) What is the difference between a hedgehog and a porcupine?

(g) In what town is the World's Fair held every year?

(h) What is the population of Stratton?

(i) Where is the Craftsbury Fiddler's Contest held?

(j) What is the difference between a Jersey and a Holstein?

(k) What is the difference between a hornpout and a bullhead?

(l) What is the difference between a buck and a doe?

(m) In what year did cows no longer outnumber people in Vermont?

(n) How many Democrats were elected Governor of Vermont between 1860 and 1960?

(o) How many gallons of sap does it take to make a gallon of syrup?

The correct answers are provided on page 90.

7

Real Vermonters Don't Ski at Stowe

Recreation is a relative thing. When you spend 10-12 hours a day in hard physical labor, you aren't inclined toward the "active sports." You don't take your vacation and climb the Presidentials, or "run Boston," or do Outward Bound, or hike the Long Trail.[1]

By the same token Real Vermonters don't ski— they don't ski at Stowe, or Killington, or Mad River, or Jay. They don't "downhill" at all. And they never ski X-C.[2]

Real Vermonters don't play golf, or sail, or soar, or play polo. They don't hit tennis balls, squash balls, or racquetballs. They don't knock heads in rugby or bodies in lacrosse.

Real Vermonters recreate carefully. They like to fish and hunt—things you can sit down and think at. Proof? Real Vermonters never share their knowledge of trout pools and deer runs.

---

[1] Real Vermonters know the Long Trail is a pathway for Flatlanders so they can see Vermont without getting lost.

[2] For the one or two Real Vermonters who may stumble into this book by accident: X-C means "cross country" in flat-landese.

Real Vermonters don't dance aerobically (or anaerobically) unless they get winded square-dancing. They don't jump out of planes for the hell of it. Real Vermonters don't pump iron or "Nautilize." History doesn't tell of any Real Vermonter who ever entered a hot tub, Jacuzzi, or sauna.

And most Real Vermonters don't swim.[3]

Real Vermonters don't jog or run . . . anywhere. If it's worth getting to, it'll be there even if you take your time.

Real Vermonters don't go on bird walks without carrying No. 7½ shot. And, Real Vermonters don't go leaf-peeping.

[3] Although that does not stop them from driving out on the ice in April.

8

Real Vermonters Don't Live in Log Cabins

(or one-room schoolhouses or old depots)

We have long known that you can judge a person's character by the character of his nest. We've found the same is true in distinguishing between Real Vermonters and Flatlanders. For instance:

Real Vermonters always refer to houses not in terms of present occupants but by the names of previous owners.

Real Vermonters don't hang oxen yokes over their garage doors.

Real Vermonters don't use solar panels,[1] Clivus Multrum toilets, or geodesic domes.

Real Vermonters don't "landscape" their yards or have Japanese maples that glow red when they should be green. They don't own Garden Way carts.

Real Vermonters don't burn wood unless they have to.[2] If Real Vermonters must burn wood, they don't

---

[1] After many years of gathering empirical evidence, Real Vermonters detected that the sun shines preciously little in Vermont. They are astounded that Flatlanders have never noticed this.

[2] Real Vermonters have found burning wood to be dirty, hard work, and bad for trees. Hefting a thermostat up two notches with an index finger, on the other hand, is no problem at all.

make comparing wood stoves a topic for conversation. They also know a fireplace is best used as an extra wastebasket.

Real Vermonters have always understood that the very best "active solar system" is a clothesline.

Real Vermonters don't take down the plastic or the banking around their foundations until June. Anyone seen mowing the lawn after September 15th is not a Real Vermonter.

Real Vermonters don't padlock ten-speed bikes to their porches.[3] They don't have Georgia O'Keefe or Andrew Wyeth prints on their walls. Nor do they put barn boards anywhere inside the house. A Real Vermonter's bed does not ebb and flow. If there is a stack of egg cartons on the refrigerator, it's a Real Vermonter's kitchen.

Real Vermonters don't have coffee tables with the following publications on them:

*Self
Fortune
Playboy
Raising Rabbits for Fun and Profit
Architectural Digest
Passages
The New Yorker
New Hampshire Profiles
Building Your Own Stone Wall
Us*

Real Vermonters do not have long driveways.[4] If there is a pickup in the driveway that does not have a gun rack, you are at the home of a Flatlander. Depending on the season, the gun rack will carry a shotgun, rifle, a fishing pole, or all three. Sometimes it carries a carpenter's level or rope. A pickup with a bumper sticker that reads "Small Farms Forever" was

---

[3]They don't own ten-speed bikes.
[4]And they don't pave the ones they have.

likely made overseas and belongs to a Flatlander. Real Vermonters' pickups proclaim: "If you outlaw guns only outlaws will have guns." If there is a man out back tearing down a barn to get a better view of the mountains, it is not a Real Vermonter's property.[5] Real Vermonters, of course, always park their cars pointing out—it's easier getting out head-first than backwards after a good snowfall.

A Doberman chained menacingly by the garage identifies a Flatlander's home. When there is a German Shepherd running free but sitting by the garage with a "take your chances" glint in his eye, it is safe to go ahead and knock if you make damn sure you knock like a Real Vermonter.

Real Vermonters don't put fences around meadows or pastures when they intend to keep no stock. And don't forget that Real Vermonters do not have pets with haircuts. They don't own cats with collars. If it slithers, flies, swims, or yips, it doesn't belong to a Real Vermonter. Real Vermonters don't wash their dogs or own Siamese cats.

Real Vermonters keep no pets of any kind inside the house at night.

Real Vermonters don't call the plumber.

Real Vermonters don't leave the lights on when they go out at night.[6]

Finally, almost no one living anywhere in the Mad River Valley or Woodstock is a Real Vermonter.

[5]Besides, Real Vermonters would never tear down a barn when they could let it fall down.

[6]Using an automatic timer to turn on the lights at dusk is the mark of a true Flatlander.

REAL VERMONTERS USE
THE RIGHT TOOL.

Real Vermonters don't expose their beams.

9

Real Vermonters Don't Drive Volvos*

Real Vermonters don't drive four-wheel drives. They buy a 1963 Chevy and throw a couple of 100 lb. Blue Seal grain bags in the trunk. Cinder blocks will do.

Real Vermonters don't boast about their mpg.[1] They don't know where their car is ranked in *Consumer Reports.*

Real Vermonters don't like PCV valves. They don't lock their gas caps. In fact, they seldom lock their cars. Real Vermonters know diesel fuel is for tractors, not automobiles. They still have not decided, however, if the craziest drivers are from Quebec or Massachusetts.

Real Vermonters don't have bumper stickers that read "Drive 55 — Stay Alive" or "Have You Hugged Your Kid Today?" or "Only Love Beats Milk" or "Save the Seals."[2]

Real Vermonters don't own motorcycles (or mopeds).

Real Vermonters don't wash their cars.[3]

*Or Saabs, Peugeots, Renaults, Audis, BMW's or Fiats.

[1]Mostly because they don't even know what it is.

[2]Real Vermonters are more interested in saving the Jersey cow from the encroachment of Holstein-mad dairy "agri-businessmen."

[3]It loosens the rust.

REAL VERMONTERS DON'T
IGNORE ROAD SIGNS.

No Real Vermonter's car brags that it "Climbed Mt. Washington."

Real Vermonters don't have vanity license plates.

There are no pickup trucks owned by Real Vermonters that do *not* have agricultural license plates on them.[4] No Real Vermonters would ever simonize their pickups. Real Vermonters don't have cars that play music when you leave the keys in the ignition. And their cars don't have retractable headlights or a windshield wiper on the back window either.[5]

Real Vermonters don't let the chain go slack when they're being towed.[6]

Real Vermonters don't "fog it," "goose it," or "rev it" when they are stuck and you're pushing by hand. They *ease* it out.

When you tell Real Vermonters to "tighten 'er up . . . slowly," they don't pop the clutch.

Real Vermonters don't grind away when the fumes would choke a horse. They know flooding when they smell it.

Real Vermonters don't like hatchbacks. They like trunks. Big trunks.

Real Vermonters don't take off their snow tires until August.[7]

Finally, Real Vermonters don't honk when the light turns green.

[4]What would happen if the Vermont Motor Vehicle Department compared the number of agricultural plates issued in Vermont to the number of farmers in Vermont?

[5]Real Vermonters (contrary to popular belief) do not go backwards that much.

[6]Real Vermonters, one should add, tow and are towed much more than Flatlanders.

[7]By then, as Real Vermonters know, snow may come at anytime anyway.

SHOW ME AN "I L♥VERMONT"
BUMPER STICKER AND I'LL SHOW
YOU A FLATLANDER.

**Real Vermonters don't
flinch
when they snap on
the jumper cables.**

10
The Real Vermont Quiz # 3

Match the items in the right-hand column with those in the left.

PART I

(1) _____ Calvin Coolidge   (A) Hubbardton
(2) _____ Seth Warner   (B) Harvey's Lake
(3) _____ Edna Beard   (C) Newbury
(4) _____ Harold Arthur   (D) "You lose."
(5) _____ Jacques Cousteau   (E) The Lone Granger
(6) _____ Orville Gibson   (F) Legislative firsts

PART II

(1) ___ 1968   (A) The Irasburg Affair
(2) ___ 1927   (B) The Defeat of Peanut Kennedy
(3) ___ 1938   (C) The Great Flood
(4) ___ 1981   (D) The Washington to Moscow Walk
(5) ___ 1974   (E) The Great Hurricane

The correct answers are provided on pages 91-93.

11

Real Vermonters Don't Shop at the Co-op

- Real Vermonters don't eat tofu, spinach linguine, or Chicken Marengo.
- Real Vermonters don't drink 2% milk or decaffeinated coffee.
- Real Vermonters plant vegetable gardens for food, not for conversation.
- Real Vermonters don't eat whole-wheat doughnuts.
- Real Vermonters don't eat yogurt.
- Real Vermonters wouldn't dream of putting Vermont Maid syrup on their pancakes.
- Real Vermonters don't grow oregano, Brussels sprouts, eggplants, or cherry tomatoes.
- Real Vermonters don't drink diet soda. Nor do they belong to the "Pepsi generation."
- Real Vermonters don't "brown bag it."
- Real Vermonters don't avoid junk food. They especially like jelly doughnuts and french fries.
- Real Vermonters never refer to a store in the country as a country store.
- Real Vermonters won't go out of their way to buy Ben and Jerry's ice cream.[1]
- Real Vermonters prefer brown eggs.
- Real Vermonters know granola is just raw oatmeal.
- Real Vermonters don't use Weber Kettles.
- Real Vermonters don't diet.

---

[1] Or eat Häagen-Dazs under any circumstances.

REAL VERMONTERS DON'T DRINK
IMPORTED BEER UNLESS THEY DO
THE IMPORTING.

12
What Real Vermonters Dread the Most

- Change
- Reappraisal
- Restrictions against shooting dogs caught chasing deer
- Power failures at chore time
- Running out of gas on a snowmobile
- August frost
- March heat
- Flatlanders with flat tires and lots of advice
- Dead batteries
- Zoning
- Running out of worms
- Gun control
- Being rushed

13
The
Real Vermonters'
All-Time Enemies List

John Kenneth Galbraith

For suggesting in a speech at the University of Vermont that Vermont was a good state to consult from but he wouldn't want to live here.

Arnold Toynbee

For claiming Vermont was "above the optimum climatic area" of the United States and therefore had made little contribution to the culture of America.

Stephen Douglas

For his remark "Vermont is the most glorious spot on the face of the globe for a man to be born in, provided he emigrates when he is very young."

The Georgia Legislature

For suggesting that "a ditch be dug around Vermont and the state be floated out to sea."

Franklin Roosevelt

For attempting to blacktop the ridgeline of the Green Mountains from Massachusetts to Canada with a huge highway called the Green Mountain Parkway.[1]

Maine

For denying Vermont the distinction of being the *only* state to vote against FDR in 1936.[2]

April

For always promising so much and delivering so little.

Whomever

For writing *Moonlight in Vermont.*

New Hampshire

For being so damned liberal.

The Vermont Development Department

For promoting the "Vermont: The Beckoning Country" campaign so effectively.

[1] Fortunately Vermonters voted it down at Town Meeting.
[2] Vermont and Maine were the only states to vote against Roosevelt in 1936. This prompted that well-known political saying "As Maine goes, so goes Vermont."

14
A Real Vermonter by Any Other Name

Sometimes you get lucky. Take the problem of identifying Real Vermonters. Sometimes the truth is in the name. For example: Reggie Winthrop? Spell it F-L-A-T-L-A-N-D-E-R. Right? No question about it. But Les Moore? Color Les "REAL VERMONTER." Here are some others:

Perly Sparrow	June Rose
Ruby Priest	Hiram Teed
Orange Roberts	Renwick Wilson
Cola Hudson	Safford Bayley
Hazen Wood	Wilbur Blodgett
Norman Sleeper	Burns Page
Mert Sage	Roscoe Bolster
Ernest Earle	Ashley Munger
Iva Lack	Royal Cutts

IN VERMONT, SEX IS NO JOKE.

15

The Real Vermonter's Kid

One way to uncover Real Vermonters these days is to find Real Vermonters' kids and then follow them home. Unlike other kids, they don't walk around plugged into radios on their belts. Sometimes you can find a Real Vermonter's kid perched on a tractor, holding up traffic on Route 7 somewhere south of Rutland.

Real Vermonters' kids can load a shotgun when they're 10, change a tire when they're 11, run a chain saw at 12, and drive a car at 13. Real Vermonters' kids don't go to summer camp unless they work there. Real Vermonters' kids like to drive like hell over dirt roads in the summer at night. Real Vermonters' kids don't take ballet or tennis lessons. A Real Vermonter's kid's favorite day is the first day of deer season (for boys) and Junior Prom night (for girls).

Real Vermonters' kids can be found in July down by the brook trying to dam it up and build a swimming hole big enough to jump into without scraping their hindsides. In the summer Real Vermonters' kids don't play basketball, and they don't start playing baseball until June. They don't play lacrosse at all.

A REAL
VERMONTER'S
KID.

In the fall you can find them ignoring the foliage almost anywhere. Any girl wearing an oversize boy's FFA jacket is a Real Vermonter's kid. Guaranteed. Real Vermonters' kids do not wear clogs. The kid you see struggling down a country road in November under a sack of butternuts that would flatten a water buffalo is a Real Vermonter's kid.

In the winter the little girl bouncing that huge snowmobile across the pasture is a Real Vermonter's kid. Real Vermonters' kids don't go skating. At the local basketball game the Real Vermonter's kid is usually on the bench, way down at the end. You can tell him by his forearms which are bigger than his biceps.

Come spring Real Vermonters' kids can be found along little brooks blowing on their hands and trying to stab a frozen night crawler with a hook they can see but can't feel. Sometimes they can be seen sitting patiently about 10 feet from a woodchuck hole. They intend to welcome the innocent little creature to spring with a blast from a 12 gauge shotgun at full choke. The woodchuck goes immediately to heaven and the Real Vermonter's kid ends up on his ass.

The 10-year-old girl jumping rope by herself in the dry part of the driveway in heavy black boots at dusk is a Real Vermonter's kid.

In spring, however, it's best to lay off looking for Real Vermonters' kids. They are tired after a long winter. They are deep in the postpartum blues of May. They sigh a lot and get sleepy and wonder if it's all worth it.

They are, after all, Real Vermonters' kids.

REAL VERMONTERS DON'T NAME
THEIR DAUGHTERS HEIDI

(or Heather, Allison, Tammy, Muffy, Vanessa, Tiffany, or Jessica.)

REAL VERMONTERS DON'T NAME
THEIR SONS SEAN

(or Joshua, Leighton, Courtenay, Zachary, Winthrop, Billy Joe, or Adrian.)

16

The Real Vermonters' Belief System

Real Vermonters believe in the Union, the American flag, and the Fourth of July. They believe in Lincoln's Birthday, but they don't believe in Groundhog Day. Real Vermonters believe in Town Meeting, ginseng, and cedar fence posts. They don't believe in the Fish and Game Department, valium, or aluminum siding.

Real Vermonters don't believe in summer.[1]

Real Vermonters have faith in December; they know it will always be cold. They have faith in June; it too will usually be cold. They distrust April and October. They like January the best because they know things can't get any worse. They hate August the most because once it comes there's nothing more to look forward to.

Real Vermonters don't believe in the last day of deer season or leash laws. To a Real Vermonter there is no redeeming social value in a magazine that has glossy pages and weighs over eight ounces.

Real Vermonters don't believe in using "impact" as a verb or "quality" as an adjective.

---

[1] They know seeing is believing.

Real Vermonters don't believe that John Stark was from New Hampshire, Ethan Allen drank too much, or the Green Mountain Boys lost the battle of Hubbardton.[2]

Real Vermonters suspect that Ethan Allen didn't demand the surrender of Fort Ticonderoga in 1775 "in the name of the Great Jehovah and the Continental Congress." But, what the hell.

Real Vermonters believe that when the work's done, it's time to find more.

Since Rusty Parker died, Real Vermonters don't believe anything they hear before seven in the morning.

Real Vermonters don't distrust all out-of-staters— just those who come from states more populous than Vermont.

Real Vermonters don't believe in taking unwanted pets away to be "put to sleep." They believe in doing the dirty work themselves.

Real Vermonters believe in barbed wire and milking machines.[3]

Real Vermonters don't believe in road salt.[4]

---

[2] Or that the Battle of Bennington was fought in New York.

[3] Show us someone milking a cow by hand and we'll show you a Flatlander.

[4] Unless it snows.

REAL VERMONTERS DON'T TRUST
CEREALS THAT MAKE NOISE.

Real Vermonters know that Vermont is bigger than Texas.

(If you flattened it out, that is.)

Real Vermonters
Don't Deal in Dishonesty
Just to be Polite

Herewith a story—

Before Coolidge left the White House, his Vermont neighbors decided to recognize his devotion to the old family farm where he had spent his boyhood by giving him a handmade rake. The orator who presented the rake in an elaborate ceremony dwelt at length on the qualities of the hickory wood from which it was made. "Hickory," he said, "like the President, is sturdy, strong, resilient, unbroken." Then he handed the rake to Coolidge and the audience settled back for his speech of acknowledgment. Coolidge turned the rake over, looked at it carefully, and said: "ASH."

Real Vermonters
Don't Indulge
in Disingenuous Greetings

A case in point—

> "Howdy, Cal!"
> "Howdy, Newt!" the man in the wagon passed
> on, waving his whip. "Cousin of mine," Vice-
> President Coolidge explained to a friend visiting
> Plymouth Notch. "Haven't seen him for twenty
> years."

How Do You Know When Real Vermonters Like You?

Only Flatlanders can know the glow that comes when they discover that a Real Vermonter LIKES them. Here are a few signs that such bliss may be near.

- They invite you in through the kitchen door.
- They don't call you before they come to visit.
- They don't ask you if you'd rather have decaffeinated coffee.
- They don't remind you to put on your snow tires.
- They don't come to visit during deer season, the first day of trout fishing, any Sunday afternoon in October, or until after the driveway dries up in April.
- They don't offer you extra vegetables from their gardens.
- When they see you they don't say "How's the family?" or "We've got to get together. Why don't you give us a call when things settle down a bit?"
- They don't call to tell you to cover your tomatoes.
- They don't offer help unless you really need it.

18

The Real Vermonter Quiz # 4

1. Which of the following is least apt to be found on a Real Vermonter's table?

   a) fiddlehead ferns
   b) cowslips
   c) dandelions
   d) bean sprouts

2. Which one of the following is most apt to be found on a Real Vermonter's table?

   a) corn silk salad
   b) clover hearts
   c) water lily shoots
   d) quiche

3. Which one of the following doesn't belong?

   a) Jeffersonville
   b) Orleans
   c) East Montpelier
   d) Wells River

4. Washington County is to Washington Town as:

   a) Addison County is to Addison Town
   b) Chittenden County is to Chittenden Town
   c) Orange County is to Orange Town
   d) Windham County is to Windham Town

The correct answers are provided on page 93.

19
Questions a Flatlander Should Never Ask a Real Vermonter

With fewer and fewer Real Vermonters around, it is possible that a Flatlander could spend almost his or her entire life in Vermont and never meet one. However, there is always the chance that a Flatlander could run into a Real Vermonter quite by accident on a snowmobile trail.[1] Therefore, it is important that a Flatlander know how to behave around the natives. The following questions provide an elementary reverse catechism—that is, questions a Flatlander should NOT ask.

- How much do you figure it's worth?
- When do we take a break?[2]
- Have you read *Real Vermonter's Don't Milk Goats*?
- How long have you lived here?
- Where is the interstate?
- How do you like Vermont?

[1]It is more likely, however, that a Flatlander will be run into by a Real Vermonter on a snowmobile trail.
[2]If you don't believe us ask Noel Perrin.

- How do you tell when they're in heat?
- Where did you go to college?
- Cold enough for ya?
- When does spring come?
- Who cleans your chimney?
- Where were you born?
- What's the bottom line?
- Where is a good place to eat in Burlington?
- Can I borrow it?
- Are you lost?[3]

[3] Real Vermonters, as Howard Mosher points out, "never get lost. They just get turned around."

20

The
Real Vermonters'
All-Time Great Quotations

"Put the Vermonters in front and keep the column
well closed up."

General John Sedgwick
at the Battle of Gettysburg

"There is no more Yankee than Polynesian in me, but
when I go to Vermont I feel like I'm traveling toward
my own place."

Bernard De Voto

"The Gods of the Hills are not the Gods of the Valleys."

Ethan Allen

"Vermont is perhaps the only place in America a
stranger can feel homesick for before he has even
left it."

Neal Pierce

"If the spirit of liberty should vanish in other parts of
the Union and support of our institutions should
vanish, it could all be replenished by the generous
store held by the people of this brave little state of
Vermont."

Calvin Coolidge

"Vermont is a country which abounds in the most active and rebellious race on the continent and hangs like a gathering storm on my left."

"Gentleman Johnny" Burgoyne

"Two classes of people are dependent on agriculture for their living. Those who live off farming and those who live off the farmers."

George Aiken

21

Things Real Vermonters Don't Comprehend

- "Exact Change" lanes
- vacations
- high tide
- snow days
- mezzanines
- megalopolis
- the "fast lane"
- bargain basements
- catching rays
- Reaganomics
- "second" homes
- "starter" houses
- est
- psychotherapy
- earrings on men
- low-cal beer
- 10K runs
- brunch
- The Bob Newhart Show

REAL VERMONTERS KNOW THE
DIFFERENCE BETWEEN A BUSINESS
AND A HOBBY.

Real Vermonters suspect that French Intensive Gardening is probably immoral.

22

Things
Real Vermonters
Are Born With

- A sense of where "north" is
- An inclination to say "no"
- Patience
- An ability to drive in the snow
- One leg shorter than the other
- A talent for telling time without a watch
- One thousand different ways to indicate the affirmative
- Knowledge about angles and leverage
- The guts to spank children when they are being little brats
- A taste for boiled greens of any kind
- An ability to tell New Hampshire from Vermont
- A dexterity for milking cows blindfolded
- No fear of the truth

23

The Real Vermonters' Politics

Flatlanders misunderstand nothing about Real Vermonters as much as they misunderstand their politics. This is because they define a Real Vermonter's politics in terms of the golden age of Republicanism in Vermont, an age that ended in 1927 with the great flood.[1] The following should help set the record straight:

a. Real Vermonters don't vote a straight party ticket.

b. Real Vermonters don't hate welfare recipients. (Vermont's record on public assistance has always equaled or surpassed that of the average American state.) They *do* hate welfare cheaters.

c. Real Vermonters don't always vote conservative. Barry Goldwater did worse in Vermont than he did nationwide in 1964, and John Anderson ran better in Vermont than in almost any other state.[2]

[1]Historians of Vermont Sam Hand and Greg Sanford have described the flood of 1927 as a "watershed" event in the state's history that "washed away" the myth of local self sufficiency (the state had to rebuild the towns' bridges) and with it a cornerstone of Republican hegemony. Their history is better than their puns.

[2]Although we therefore suspect there were some Real Vermonters who actually voted for Lyndon Johnson in 1964 and for John Anderson in 1980, we have yet to discover one who will own up to it.

d. Real Vermonters have always elected more women and fewer lawyers to the state legislature than the voters in other states have.

TOWN MEETING

Real Vermonters don't like the Australian ballot or Town Meetings held at night. Real Vermonters know any damn fool can speak his piece at Town Meeting, and they therefore don't speak out too often. Flatlanders at Town Meetings usually wait several years before they make damn fools of themselves.[3] Anyone at Town Meeting that prefaces his or her remarks with "I would like to discuss . . ." or ends them with "Thank you very much" is not a Real Vermonter. At Town Meetings Real Vermonters are more apt to "call the question." Real Vermonters know the most important politician in town is the Town Clerk.[4]

The Real Vermonter's favorite warning item is: "To vote $100.00 for the observance of Memorial Day."[5] The most unpopular item: "To see if the Town will adopt a uniform auditing system as recommended by

[3] Want to hear about a Flatlander crybaby? Read the *Burlington Free Press* of March 27, 1983 where a Californian whined that he had lived in Vermont almost a year and wasn't sure he was liked yet. Real Vermonters won't indulge this behavior. They know that before this fellow has any chance of becoming a Real Vermonter he has to cross that first great plateau and say truthfully, "I don't give a damn if my neighbors like me or not." Meanwhile he'll have to be patient for a decade or so. Real Vermonters know neighborliness is not invoked by physical proximity. It comes with the seasons and is all the more valuable for it.

[4] The Town Clerk is very often a woman.

[5] After 3:00 p.m. the most favorite item becomes adjournment.

the State." The most feared event at Town Meeting for a Real Vermonter is a Flatlander standing and clearing his or her throat anytime after 4:00 p.m.

POLITICS

In politics Real Vermonters don't like:
- The closed primary
- The four-year term
- Legislature still in session after trout season opens
- Out-of-state contributions
- Politicians who change parties[6]

The Real Vermonter's most respected politician of the century: George Aiken.

The Real Vermonter's most despised politician of the century: Joe McCarthy

The campaign technique most distrusted by Real Vermonters in this century: Stewart Ledbetter's second walk through the state in 1982.

The second most distrusted campaign technique: Stewart Ledbetter's first walk through Vermont in 1980.

The Real Vermonter's least liked Presidential candidate: Teddy Kennedy.

The Real Vermonter's least liked decision of the General Assembly: Turning the deer herd over to the Fish and Game Department.

The future campaign act most dreaded by Real Vermonters: a third walk by Stewart Ledbetter.

[6]John Connally comes to mind.

A REAL VERMONT FARMER
IS SOMEONE WHO STANDS UP
AT TOWN MEETING AND IDENTIFIES
HIMSELF AS A FARMER . . .

AND NOBODY GRINS.

A REAL VERMONTER
TOWN MEETING TALE

By John McClaughry

"I'm from southern Illinois originally. At my second town meeting in Kirby I was elected moderator of the Town Meeting. (This was a fluke—I was the only candidate present.) I was very surprised and nervous but managed to stumble through the morning session. In line for lunch my confidence was swelled immensely when I overheard a review of my performance spoken in an approving tone, 'Ain't from around here, but he's a hick from somewhere.'"

24

The Real Vermonters' Political Awards

THE BEST BUREAUCRATIC BULL
OF THE POST-WAR ERA

The Vermont Fish and Game Department[1]

THE MOST APPRECIATED WHITE LIE
OF THE POST-WAR ERA

Former Governor Deane Davis[2]

TOASTMASTER OF THE YEAR AWARD

T. Garry Buckley[3]

[1] For claiming that the statewide slaughter of thousands of does and fawns in 1979, 1980, 1981, and 1982 was a "planned *harvest* of 'antlerless deer.' "

[2] For arguing during his campaign for Governor in 1968 that he wasn't *really sure* if he would try to institute a sales tax if elected.

[3] For two of the best one-liners ever delivered by a Vermont politician:

"A Real Vermonter's Seven-Course Meal is a six-pack of beer and a jacked deer steak."

"Even a blind hog will find an acorn once in a while."

THE MOST CONVOLUTED

POLITICAL DECISION

Jim Jeffords[4]

___

THE MOST EMBARRASSING POLITICAL

ACT TO REAL VERMONTERS

Bernie Sanders[5]

___

THE MOST APPRECIATED POLICY

RECOMMENDATION OF THE POST-WAR ERA

George Aiken[6]

[4]Congressman Jim, who wants so much to be a Senator, lost his nerve and didn't challenge freshman Senator Pat Leahy in 1980 assuming that Senator Stafford would retire and he would step easily into his seat in 1982. This led to the Real Vermonter's most famous *"damn"* of the post-war era when Stafford refused to retire and Jim was trapped in his House seat for at least another four years waiting to get the chance to run against Leahy who would, of course, be a much stronger incumbent.

[5]After decades of the erosion of local autonomy, Real Vermonters were shamefaced that it took a socialist from New York City to stand up to the legislature and demand an increase in the powers of the localities.

[6]When he suggested that we resolve the dilemma of extricating ourselves from the Vietnam War by declaring victory and leaving.

THE DON QUIXOTE AWARD

Peter Diamondstone[7]

THE MOST RIDICULOUS

SUPREME COURT DECISION

Baker vs. Carr[8]

[7]Peter has run for statewide office six times in the last seven elections: three times for Attorney General (averaging 2.7% of the vote) and three times for the U.S. Congress (averaging 5.0% of the vote). We congratulate you for beating out Morris Earle of New Haven, the "Small is Beautiful" candidate, in 1982 by a 1.69% to 1.05% margin. Perhaps if you expand your political base to a wider spectrum of the electorate than is represented by junkyard dealers you would do better. Anyway, a Real Vermonter "go for it" to you in 1984.

[8]This led to reapportionment of the State's House of Representatives and gave Chittenden County its rightful number of seats. It used to be that the Northeast Kingdom had 49 members and Chittenden County had 17. Now Chittenden County has 33 and the Kingdom has 16. What Real Vermonter would like that? Real Vermonters trusted the math but they didn't trust the politics.

25

Items Not Found
in a Real Vermonter's
General Store

The New York Times
Breath sweeteners
Decaf espresso beans
Suntan oil
Heineken beer
Stoned Wheat Thins
Fish of any kind
"Real" peanut butter
Real Vermonters Don't Milk Goats
Automatic chain saw sharpeners
Fresh mushrooms
A cracker barrel
Native corn
Self magazine
Goldfish food
Rubber dishwashing gloves
Plastic trash bags
Real tea leaves
Piña colada mix
Duo-fold underwear
Weed eaters
Contact lens fluid
Artichoke hearts
Plastic worms

A "REAL" COUNTRY STORE?
☐ TRUE ☐ FALSE

**Real Vermonters don't buy
their Christmas trees at
supermarkets.**

26
Who Are
Real Vermonters?

It is time to fish or cut bait. The sky may threaten but the hay needs cutting. While dancing around the edges telling you what Real Vermonters are NOT, we have been skimpy in our descriptions of what they ARE.

Our dilemma springs from the fact that there are precious few Real Vermonters left. Oh sure, you can say that so and so is a Real Vermonter because he or she was born here. But that's a cop out. Any damn fool knows that Stubb Earle, Dick Mallary, Madeline Harwood, Sadie White, Deane Davis, Susan Webb, and Sandra Dragon are Real Vermonters. But if mere birth did a Real Vermonter make, the State would be poor in genes as well as income.

Even if we were armed with perfect categories, however, placing *real* people in them would be, like logging in the wind, very ticklish business indeed. Yet most would agree that Vermont, like Texas, is more than just a place—it's a state of mind. Vermonters are committed to a certain creed and live by certain values that set them apart. Some people have them. Others do not. Most are somewhere in between. Yet social critics often are content to divide the world into two classes— Real Vermonters and Flatlanders.

Through painstaking, brain-crunching research we have expanded this simplistic dichotomy into the following precise classifications worthy of Linnaeus.

VERMONT LEANERS[1]

These people land close, but because of some personality quirk, or other deformity, they are simply not ringers.

Dick Snelling

Poor Governor Snelling. For years he's let people walk all over him. Real Vermonters aren't afraid to speak their minds! Take a course in Assertiveness Training, Dick.[2]

Phil Hoff

Not until he publicly disavows the statement often attributed to him that he "brought Vermont kicking and screaming into the 20th Century" can he be a Real Vermonter.

Peter Smith

"We feel a need to unpack this one and try to get in touch with our own feelings before we begin the word crafting." Sound familiar, Peter? Stop talking like a Flatlander and you could become a Real Vermonter.

Bernie Sanders

The Mayor of Burlington must (1) renounce socialism, (2) shed his accent, (3) promise never to run for higher office.

[1]As in horsehoes (a Real Vermonter's game), close counts in this book.

[2]You need not go back to the University of Havana, however.

VERMONT TWEENERS

This category includes people who show some distinct capacity to become Real Vermonters but they equivocate on everything except finding the middle ground.

Jim Jefords

Congressman Jeffords can't decide if he's a Republican or a Democrat, wants to be a Senator or Governor, or where to sleep at night—in his office or in a house like Real Vermonters do.

Madeleine Kunin

No one with the nickname "Straddlin' Madeleine" could possibly be a Real Vermonter.

Sister Elizabeth Candon

Anyone, even a Pittsford native, caught between Governor Snelling and Bishop John Marshall without trying to squirm free could not be anything but a "tweener."

REAL VERMONTER WAITING LIST

This is a long one as hundreds of outsiders line up to apply for Real Vermonter status or bask in the reflected glory of Real Vermonters.

John Irving

He must stop wrestling and posing on magazine covers. Real Vermonters don't wrestle after the age of 14.

George Bush

He's on everybody's waiting list.

John Glenn

He has many of the qualities Real Vermonters admire most. But we're not sure he has "the right stuff" to become a Real Vermonter.

Grizzly Adams

Grizzly is on the list because he's the person most people in Hackensack and Nashville think Real Vermonters look like.

Muhammad Ali

For his courage, commitment to principle, sense of humor, and honesty, Ali is high on this list. He has only to apologize for making Howard Cosell famous and he's in.

Jeane Kirkpatrick

Anything to get her out of the U.N.

Tommy Hahn

All you have to do is come back from Montana, Tommy, and apologize to Dick Snelling.[3]

NATIVE FLATLANDERS

These people had everything going for them (for example, they were born in Vermont), and they still blew it. Some of their number would divide up the

---

[3]Apologize for what? For publicly calling the Governor the most awful word in the Real Vermonter's vocabulary. Hahn called Snelling a FL——————ER.

family farm into quarter-acre lots and call the development "Moonlight Acres."

Pat Leahy

Vermont's junior Senator in Washington tries too hard. Real Vermonters are tired of hearing about the "farm back in Middlesex."

Bob Stafford

Vermont's senior Senator was ever so close to a tenured Real Vermontership (despite his long addiction to "tweenerism") until Robert Redford campaigned for him in 1982.

Jack Barry

A Real Vermonter knows when to stop talking.

PERPETUAL ASPIRANTS

These are Flatlanders who want desperately to be like Real Vermonters. Many are sweet, kind, and very sincere. But they just can't seem to shake their flatlanderism.

Jim Guest

Jim, move out of Waitsfield and stop trying to "aw shucks it." If you are to ever win another statewide election in Vermont you must remember, "You can put the boy in the country but you can't put the country in the boy."

Jerry Diamond

Disappear into the Northeast Kingdom for a decade. Cut pulp for John McClaughry if he'll have you. When you emerge talking like a Real Vermonter, people will be less apt to chuckle.

Stewart Ledbetter

Take your next walk on the long trail and jaw with the chipmunks.

Jim Mullin

We know you love your wife. Real Vermonters wonder about those who find it necessary to announce it in public *so* damned often.

THE REAL VERMONTER BENCH

These people make the team. They are good solid, reliable Real Vermonters. They hustle, come to all the practices, have tons of heart, and give you 101% all the time. Unfortunately, we just can't start 'em because they weren't born here.

Jim Douglas	Charlie Morrissey
Em Hebard	Henry Carse
John Downs	Sterry Waterman
Herb Ogden	Brendan Whittaker
Betty Bandel	Lyman Rowell

INSTANT VERMONTERS

Once in every century or so a Flatlander comes along who epitomizes the best of the Real Vermonter. Between his soul and the spirit of the state there is an instant match. Such a person is:

Aleksandr Solzhenitsyn

REAL VERMONTERS

This category should be self explanatory, but it isn't. Trouble is most of the people we all know as Real Vermonters are not public figures since Real Vermonters are too busy being Real Vermonters. The quintessential exception that proves the rule is:

George Aiken

Any listing of Real Vermonters is, of course, a personal thing. Here's what we think. Who's on your list.

BRYAN'S LIST	MARES'S LIST
David Bryan	Joseph Bedor
Buster and Florence Carbee	Charlie Lawrence
Charlie Cole	Joe Monteith
Goodwin Crosby	Charles Nichols
Jason Wark	Harold Penniman
Isabel Whitney	Pearl Wilson

YOUR LIST

_____   _____

_____   _____

_____   _____

27

A Few Words About Real Vermont Women

Recently, a Real Vermont Woman, Bethel-born Susan Wertheimer, was asked while filling out forms before the birth of her second child: "Will there be a 'support person' in attendance?"

"No," she replied, "but my husband will be there."[1]

Real Vermonters are often bemused by the so-called "battle of the sexes." What does it matter if a woman sometimes wears a skirt so long as she can drive the truck? When you live on a slice of forested, frozen granite south of Canada and north of Boston, with too much to do in a day, sex distinctions blur.

In fact, there are few things Real Vermont men do that Real Vermont women don't do. For the few male chauvinists (of either sex) left in Vermont, however, we list below a few observations about Real Vermont Women:

- Real Vermont Women are damned good shots.
- A Real Vermont Woman's food processor doesn't whir or buzz. It sweats.
- Real Vermont Women don't apologize for wearing aprons.
- Real Vermont Women don't read books on child rearing or agonize over it.[2]

---

[1] Real Vermont women think Lamaze is some guy who runs a feed store in Orleans.

[2] Dr. Spock is okay for ailments, however.

- Real Vermont Women can't face spring without a little horseradish.
- The EMT of the local rescue squad is likely to be a Real Vermont Woman.
- A Real Vermont Woman may not lobby for the ERA, but she isn't afraid of it either.
- Real Vermont Women know the "Women's Auxiliary" is anything but.
- Real Vermont Women don't go to Tupperware parties or sell Mary Kay.[3]
- Real Vermont Women grow Real Vermont flowers such as phlox, lilies, and peonies, but they don't mess with Valeriana, Tradescantia, or Physostegia.
- Real Vermont Women don't Jazzercise or wear ties.
- Real Vermont Women don't put disposable diapers on their kids.[4]
- Real Vermont Women know leashes and harnesses are for animals not kids.
- Real Vermont Women don't blanche when a car dealer says, "It's a stick shift."
- Real Vermont Women don't audit courses. They take them.
- Real Vermont Women don't need a law to tell them to buckle up their kids.
- Real Vermont Women don't clean fish unless they catch them.
- The Real Vermont Woman's favorite holiday is the first day of deer season.

[3]They have been known to be Avon ladies, however.
[4]Unless they're at Town Meeting, Little League, Traffic Court, the Tunbridge Fair, an auction, or out doing the shopping or the milking.

REAL VERMONTERS DON'T MAKE PETS
OUT OF ANYTHING THEY CAN EAT.

28

Things Real Vermonters Recognize as a Waste of Time

- I-91 north of St. Johnsbury
- Shoveling out right after a snowstorm
- Planting melons
- Hoping for an early Town Meeting adjournment
- Grading the washboards
- Voting Liberty Union
- I-91 south of St. Johnsbury
- Advising a Flatlander not to burn white birch

29
It's a Fine Line

Vermont is a land of fine lines—the lines between winter and spring, hard and soft maple, well-grazed and over-grazed. Not much separates a good sugar day from a bad one, ripe apples from over-ripe, snow from freezing rain. It's a fine line between Vermont and New Hampshire (Thank God for the Connecticut River!), northern and southern Vermont, between a legal and an illegal trout, or between dusk and dark when you're waiting for a buck.

Our subject has been Real Vermonters, and we've found the "fine line" applies to people even more than to seasons, scenery, or sugaring. It's a fine line between politeness and rudeness, between humor and ridicule, between public and private, between neighborliness and intrusion, between the real and the superficial.

And . . . for all the apparently clear-cut differences between Real Vermonters and Flatlanders, every year the fence between them grows more rickety. We have tried to freeze a frame of Vermont life, to halt for an instant the narrowing of distinction between Real Vermonters and the rest of the world.

Now, God knows we don't want to preach. But if you want to get to the core of Real Vermonters, you need to know what they believe in. That's why we saved this for last.

Between Mares's skeptical Anglicanism and Bryan's shaky Catholicism, we didn't have very solid theological footing. Therefore, we have consulted with Frank's brother, David,[1] a Catholic priest, Scudder Parker, a Congregational minister in East St. Johnsbury, and Thomas Bassett, a Quaker Meeting clerk. All three have lived most of their lives in Vermont. What you have below is a well-cooked stew of their ideas and ours. The three are men of God and blameless for the result.

All people create God in their own image, and Real Vermonters are no exception.

The Real Vermonter's God is powerful and hard, but not capricious. He is fair but unforgiving—those that get it probably had it coming.

Real Vermonters believe that there are great unknowns out there and that when you put them together they add up to God.

Real Vermonters think that no one set of Christians is better than any other set. Therefore, everybody within a convenient geographical area should put up with the same preacher and the same hard pews. Congregationalism taught this, and thus it became the state religion of Vermont. Nowadays there are many denominations in Vermont, but most of the members are still Congregationalists at heart.

Real Vermonters don't need to be in church to pray. On the other hand, they don't take to TV preaching either. That's *too* comfortable.

Real Vermonters believe in original sin—sort of. Actually they believe in original stupidity, most often found in Flatlanders who are sure they've got a faster,

[1]Unlike Frank, Dave is a Real Vermonter born in Windsor, not across the river in Hanover. "Mom always liked David best."

easier, better way of doing things. When the Flatlander takes the tractor on a shortcut across the "damp" spot in the field (and has to get pulled out), a certain set comes to the Real Vermonter's jaw which says he is wrestling with that ancient curse—boneheadedness.

Real Vermonters believe religion has mostly to do with respect.

Real Vermonters don't believe anyone ever goes to heaven by talking. They don't call on God unless they need him. This may be sloppy theology, but it's easier on God. He knows that when He hears from a Real Vermonter, He's really wanted.

The quintessential real Vermont parable goes like this:

A farmer has just finished the morning milking. On his way back to the house for breakfast, he pauses to look at the sunrise. In a handful of minutes the eastern sky passes from pink to salmon to orange and finally to blazing white as the sun heaves over the mountains.

"Sure is beautiful," murmurs his wife, who has joined him.

The farmer says nothing. He remains silent throughout breakfast. Halfway through his second cup of coffee, he looks at her and says:

"YUP, AND WE'LL PAY FOR IT, TOO."

For us, that says it all.

Finally, before you get pretensions about how "real" you are, we caution you to remember that . . .

REAL VERMONTERS DON'T
READ BOOKS LIKE THIS.

Answers to the Real Vermonter Quizzes

QUIZ NUMBER ONE

(a) When a town lets a town road return to nature.
(b) Another term for a peavy.
(c) The list of issues to be discussed at a Town Meeting.
(d) When a cow calves or "comes in."
(e) A crossbar, pivoted at the middle, to which the traces of a harness are fastened for pulling a cart, carriage, or plow.
(f) The list of the value of local property gathered for purposes of taxation.
(g) A patented ointment made in Lyndonville and used as a salve for sore udders and chapped lips.
(h) A wide flatbed of planks dragged behind a horse or tractor onto which a farmer throws or rolls stones when he's "pickin' stone."
(i) The tragedy of having no sons to leave the place to.
(j) Working your ass off.
(k) A cow with one bad teat. Better than a two-titter.
(l) When a "know-it-all" Flatlander buys wood from a Real Vermonter and gets less wood than a full cord.
(m) Vermont's practice of electing governors from one side of the Green Mountains or the other on a rotating basis.
(n) George Aiken
(o) As they say . . . the first two guesses don't count.
(p) The second crop of hay in a season.

(q) A barrel stave with a seat for a Real Vermonter's kid to "sit-down" ski.
(r) A permit that allows one doe to be shot by each "party" of deer hunters.

Number wrong _____. Enter this number on page 94.

QUIZ NUMBER TWO

(a) The liberal definition is the counties of Orleans, Caledonia, and Essex. Real Vermonters, however, know that the Kingdom does not exist west of Route 5 or south of St. Jay.
(b) It depends on who's buying it.
(c) Onion River
(d) In a jail in Vergennes
(e) St. Albans
(f) To a Real Vermonter there is no difference. Flatlanders know there are no real hedgehogs in Vermont.
(g) Tunbridge. If you didn't get this one you're in real trouble.
(h) 122 Real Vermonters and 122,000 skiers
(i) Hardwick
(j) One gives real milk. Real Vermonters do not agree on which.
(k) The difference is the same as that between a mudworm and a fishworm.
(l) It depends on how dark it is or how fast they're running.
(m) Cows never outnumbered people in Vermont. Cattle did. Real Vermonters know that "cows" and "calves," and "beef" and "heifers" are not the same.
(n) None
(o) 40

Number wrong _____. Enter this number on page 94.

1. (D) ("You lose.") Famous joke about Calvin Coolidge. A vivacious, talkative lady who was to sit next to the President at a dinner party took a wager from a friend that she could not "get three words out of the President all evening." To win the bet she laughingly told Coolidge about it at dinner. Solemnly he turned to her and said, "You lose."

2. (A) (Hubbardton) Seth Warner conducted a rear guard action at Hubbardton where the Green Mountain Boys stymied British forces in pursuit of a Colonial army, recently driven from Fort Ticonderoga. Real Vermonters know that this was the first "domino" in the eventual defeat of the British. Because of it, Burgoyne lost at Saratoga. This led to the entrance of the French into the war, the Battle of Yorktown, and eventual American victory. This is one way Vermont determined the history of the galaxy, according to Real Vermonters.

3. (F) (Legislative firsts) Edna Beard was the first woman elected to Vermont's House of Representatives (1920) and later was the first woman elected to the Vermont Senate (1922).

4. (E) (The Lone Granger) Harold Arthur was one of Vermont's most colorful politicians. In 1958 he suffered the embarrassment of being the first Republican to lose a statewide race to a Democrat since 1853. He was known for his affiliation with the Vermont Grange and for his ability to whistle *The Star-Spangled Banner.*

5. (B) (Harvey's Lake) Jacques Cousteau got his start diving here. He was allegedly such a troublemaker at summer camp that he was assigned

the task of cleaning sticks from under the water at the beach at Harvey's Lake in Barnet, Vermont.

6. (C) (Newbury) In 1958 Orville Gibson was bound hand and foot and thrown into the Connecticut River from a bridge in Newbury. So began Vermont's most infamous unsolved murder. Numerous national magazine reports and two novels have been published on the murder.

PART II

1. (A) 1968 (The Irasburg Affair) Vermonters shotgunned the home of a black minister in this Orleans County town.

2. (C) 1927 (The Great Flood) In 1927 Vermont's worst natural disaster killed 84 people and caused $30,000,000 of damage.

3. (E) 1938 (The Great Hurricane) Most hurricanes head out to sea before they reach the mouth of the Connecticut in southern New England, a natural pathway north to Vermont. This one didn't.

4. (D) 1981 (Washington to Moscow Walk) In 1981 a group of peace activists walked from Washington (Vermont) to Moscow (Vermont) to demonstrate the need for international cooperation in the nuclear freeze movement.

5. (B) 1974 (The Defeat of "Peanut" Kennedy) Colorful, rural Republican Walter Kennedy of Chelsea, one of the last Real Vermonter politicians, bit the dust,

losing a race for governor to Tom Salmon, a Democratic out-of-stater, and a Catholic (of all things).[1]

Number wrong _____. Enter this number on page 94.

QUIZ NUMBER FOUR

1. (d) Bean sprouts. (If you missed this one you have a lot of work to do on becoming a Real Vermonter.)
2. (d) Quiche. (Whatdidya think? Real Vermonters would eat stuff they wouldn't feed a cow?)
3. (c) East Montpelier. All the rest are villages *within* towns. East Montpelier is the only one that's a Real Town.
4. (b) Washington Town is not in Washington County. Chittenden Town is not in Chittenden County.

Number wrong _____. Enter this number on page 94.

[1]In that campaign, Kennedy lambasted one Democratic House candidate in St. Johnsbury for being afraid to use her "real name." The woman shot back that she *was* using her real name, Chris Hadsel, and she allowed her husband, Bill Mares, to use his real name, too.

31

Are You a Real Vermonter?

SCORING THE REAL

VERMONTER QUIZZES

DIRECTIONS: Add up the total number wrong on all four quizzes.

Quiz #1: _____

Quiz #2: _____

Quiz #3: _____

Quiz #4: _____

Total wrong _____

INTERPRETING YOUR SCORE: 0-12 wrong: a Real Vermonter. 13-24 wrong: a Leaning Real Vermonter. 25-36 wrong: a Leaning Flatlander. 37-48 wrong: a Flatlander.